BROCK LESNAR

AY WYATT

UNDERTAKER

TRIPLE THREAT MATCH

BATISTA   DANIEL BRYAN   RANDY ORTON

CONTENTS

The expectation surrounding 2014's *WrestleMania XXX* has been beyond that of any other, and the action that the Superstars delivered on the night more than lived up to the hype! With opening appearances from Dwayne 'The Rock' Johnson, Hulk Hogan and Stone Cold Steve Austin, and with matches between some of the biggest, boldest, most popular Superstars in WWE history, each clash for WWE Championship success brought with it an immense amount of exhilarating excitement, sudden shocks and WWE upsets!

Within this *WrestleMania* match-book you will find some of the most electrifying key moments within each Superstar battle; the moves that turned the tide on some of the so-called 'sure thing' wins, and images of both the losers in their defeat and the victors, doused in WWE glory! Re-cap these legendary matches at your leisure and relive the moments that made this *WrestleMania* quite possibly the best the WWE Universe has ever seen!

£7.99

HEIGHT: 5'10"

WEIGHT: 210 lbs.

FROM: Aberdeen, Wa.

SIGNATURE MOVE: "Yes!" Lock

CAREER HIGHLIGHTS: WWE World Heavyweight Champion; WWE Champion; WWE Tag Team Champion; World Heavyweight Champion; United States Champion; 2011 SmackDown Money in the Bank winner

DANIEL BRYAN

Despite the odds, Daniel Bryan came to *WrestleMania XXX* and showed the WWE Universe just how capable he was of taking on the best and coming out on top! In an action packed, high-flying, brutal battle of wits and superior stamina Bryan fought through the pain of his injured shoulder to show Triple H the skills that have secured him a legion of followers since his introduction to WWE. In a battle which is sure to be remembered for years to come, the leader of the "Yes!" Movement left no doubt in the minds of his critics that he is indeed the real deal!

TRIPLE H

There's no question that Triple H deserves a huge amount of respect within the WWE Universe. With a history of wins over some of the biggest names that have ever graced the WWE arena his skills and sheer brute strength can never be called into question. During this ruthless battle of bone crunching Pedigrees, thundering clotheslines and seriously heavy suplexes, Triple H was eventually undone by the relative newcomer, his anger at losing made clear to all when he attacked a distracted Bryan after already losing the match. Triple H may not have won this one but you can be sure he'll already be planning revenge.

Adorned in Gold as every true Champion should be!

Here he comes – the King of Kings, Triple H!

Triple H couldn't look less phased; confidence oozes out of his every pore and, with wins over almost every big name in WWE, who could blame him!

The blue collar Daniel Bryan laps up the adorning crowd's chants as he prepares for battle!

And here comes the challenger, Daniel Bryan, to a deafening roar of 'Yes!' from the crowd!

Stephanie gives Triple H a kiss for luck!

The two Superstars stare each other down, neither one willing to accept the possibility of defeat!

Bryan kicks away Triple H's hand and goes immediately onto the offensive.

The King of King offers his hand to Bryan, and the crowd yells 'No'!

Taking him to the ground, Bryan goes for an instant pin... but Triple H has no trouble getting out of it.

Once back to their feet the two Superstars grapple, with Triple H backing Bryan into the corner.

Bryan counters by turning The Game in the corner and landing a number of vicious kicks to his body.

Bryan lands a massive kick, knocking H off his feet and forcing him to roll under the ropes and out of danger.

Triple H, back in the ring, shows no mercy and goes immediately for Bryan's injured shoulder.

Despite in obvious pain, Bryan manages another take down and traps his opponent in a headlock.

Triple H escapes but not for long as Daniel Bryan unleashes a flying kick into The King of Kings.

Daniel Bryan then climbs to the top rope, launches himself from it and lands heavily on Triple H, injuring both Superstars as they hit the ground.

The two Superstars lie in agony on the floor of the arena as crowds look on in disbelief.

With both men injured from the fall, Bryan attempts to mount the turnbuckle once more as a dazed Triple H clings to the ropes.

Again Triple H goes for Bryan's injured arm and the pain it causes the challenger is clear to see.

Daniel Bryan fights back, landing a number of big punches of his own

With Bryan still reeling from H's pin attempt, he's thrown into the turnbuckle and smashed with a number of punches from Triple H's huge fists.

Then, whilst Triple H stands stunned in the center of the ring, Bryan flies off the ropes and hits him with a massive forearm to the face!

Both Superstars are down and obviously feeling the effects of this punishing, epic battle!

Getting to his feet first, Bryan unleashes multiple vicious kicks to Triple H's abdomen...

...then slams him with a well-timed suplex!

Triple H battles back with a well-executed cross face chicken wing...

Triple H tries to prize Bryan from the turnbuckle, in order to perform a super-plex, but Bryan turns the tables on him with a power-mount off the second rope.

With ferocious speed and power Daniel Bryan launches a massive flying kick at Triple H, connecting solidly with his jaw!

The two Superstars pull them selves from the canvas and battle on, with Bryan climbing to the top of the turnbuckle and launching himself onto the downed Triple H.

Triple H responds by clotheslining Bryan and almost taking his head clean off!

After submission attempts by both Superstars Triple H wearily climbs out of the ring, only to turn and find Bryan flying through the ropes towards him!

After beating up Triple H some more, Bryan throws him back inside the ring, climbs to the top rope and hits him with a massive flying kick!

Triple H fights back but a brutal flying knee knocks him flying to the ground. Bryan then sees his chance, goes for the pin and, to the shock of the whole WWE arena, pins his massive opponent!

Despite Triple H's un-sportsman-like behaviour, and despite Daniel Bryan's damaged shoulder, the leader of The "Yes!" Movement recovers and lifts his arm in victory, claiming his legendary win over The King of Kings!

SETH ROLLINS

HEIGHT: 6'1"
WEIGHT: 217 lbs.
FROM: Davenport, Iowa
SIGNATURE MOVE: Peace of Mind

DEAN AMBROSE

HEIGHT: 6'4"
WEIGHT: 225 lbs.
FROM: Cincinnati, Ohio
SIGNATURE MOVE: Dirty Deeds

ROMAN REIGNS

HEIGHT: 6'3"
WEIGHT: 265 lbs.
FROM: Pensacola, Fla.
SIGNATURE MOVE:
Spear

THE SHIELD™

SETH ROLLINS

As the first ever NXT Champion, Seth Rollins made his mark quickly in WWE, but now that he's joined forces with Dean Ambrose and Roman Reigns, to form The Shield', his Superstar status is greater than ever! It's no surprise that within his role in this epic battle Rollins dished out massive punishment on The New Age Outlaws, supporting his team mates in ensuring victory, and doing his bit in making *WrestleMania XXX* one of the best *WrestleManias* ever

DEAN AMBROSE

Dean Ambrose came to *WrestleMania* with only victory on his mind. With his loyal team 'The Shield', Ambrose cemented a memorable victory over The New Age Outlaws, producing spectacular entertainment for the WWE Universe to enjoy. By proving his ability to both absorb and administer punishment to equal degree, The Shield's frontman's dedication and resolve at *WrestleMania XXX* is a testament to a career that really does stand out

ROMAN REIGNS

Roman Reigns went into the Mercedes-Benz Superdome with a look of pure belief and determination on his face, and with two potentially legendary Tag Team partners backing him up, who could blame him? From the off Reigns was a key figure in this impressive battle, hitting The New Age Outlaws with everything he had! Something tells me the Outlaws will be having nightmares about this man, due to this match, for a long time to come!

ROAD DOGG

HEIGHT: 6'1"
WEIGHT: 241 lbs.
FROM: Marietta, Ga.
SIGNATURE MOVE: Shake, Rattle and Roll

BILLY GUNN

HEIGHT: 6'3"
WEIGHT: 260 lbs.
FROM: Orlando, Fla.
ALIAS: Rockabilly

KANE

HEIGHT: 7'0"
WEIGHT: 323 lbs.
SIGNATURE MOVE: Chokeslam
ALIAS: The Big Red Monster,
The Devil's Favourite Demon

THE NEW AGE OUTLAWS ™

ROAD DOGG

This 'New Age Outlaw', along with partner in crime, Billy Gunn, is a veteran of WWE who, during his years in sports-entertainment, has picked up not only the WWE Tag Team Championship, but also the World Tag Team Championship, Intercontinental Championship, and Hardcore Championship! He and his partner, Billy Gunn, are the most decorated Tag Team in WWE history! This didn't aid the outlaws tonight however, as The Shield took them apart from the start!

BILLY GUNN

Having won 11 Tag Team titles, the Intercontinental Championship and the 1999 King of the Ring tournament since arriving on the scene in WWE, nobody can talk trash about this particular Superstar! WrestleMania XXX was not to be the Outlaw's night however, with The Shield teaching him and his Tag Teammates a few very hard, 'New Age', lessons! This veteran of WWE may have lost this one but be sure of one thing... he will be back!

KANE

Seven feet tall and weighing 300 pounds, this monster of a man must have made the hairs on the back of The Shield's neck stand up on end when he walked out into the Arena. If The Shield were intimidated, they certainly didn't show it as they slowly wore the big man down until he was no use to Gunn and Dogg! Although beginning this electrifying match in monstrous style, Kane soon tired and The Shield were able to claim victory as theirs!

Kane leads The New Age Outlaws into the arena, and the fury in his eyes is clear to see!

Billy Gunn and Road Dogg announce their arrival to the WWE arena.

As The New Age Outlaws and Kane approach the ring, a menacing air fills the arena.

But then comes The Shield, masked and even more menacing than their adversaries!

As the bell rings Ambrose taunts Kane and The Big Red Monster loses no time in getting to grips with the smaller man.

The strength of Kane becomes immediately apparent to The Shield's front man.

Roman Reigns tags in and lands a massive elbow on Billy Gunn...

...sending him crashing to the canvas!

Road Dogg then attempts to take out Reigns, but is skillfully dodged by the black-clad Superstar!

Without even a pause, Reigns then hands out a huge clothesline on Road Dogg, flooring the Superstar... hard!

Having smashed both Billy Gunn and Road Dogg into the turnbuckle, Reigns then pulls off a magnificent kick to the heads of both men.

Despite this early beating, Kane regains his composure and grabs Reigns around the throat.

Reigns isn't in trouble for long, as Rollins launches himself from the ropes and onto the unsuspecting Kane!

Rollins doesn't stop there however, somersaulting over the ropes and crashing into the visibly shocked Kane...

Kane never saw that coming! Once down he rolls out under the ropes, in order to regain his senses.

Reigns lands a massive shoulder block on Gunn...

...then lands a huge Superman punch, which puts Gunn on the canvas.

The concern on Billy Gunn's face is clear to see as he is suddenly surrounded by The Shield. He needs help... fast!

With outstanding teamwork, Ambrose and Rollins launch themselves through the ropes…

…and take out the recovering Road Dogg and Billy Gunn in brutal style…

Once back in the ring, Reigns performs a double spear…

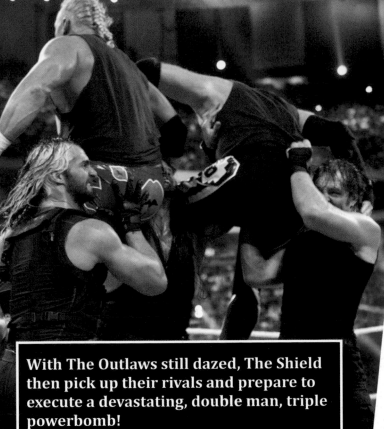

With The Outlaws still dazed, The Shield then pick up their rivals and prepare to execute a devastating, double man, triple powerbomb!

Defenceless and exhausted, Gunn and Dogg await their fate...

... which comes with swift and powerful force!

Dazed and confused, The Outlaws lie motionless as the crowd goes wild!

As Reigns already celebrates, Seth Rollins pins a stunned Billy Gunn to win the match.

A defiant Ambrose soaks up this spectacular WrestleMania XXX win...

... then climbs the ropes and sends out a message to any wannabe Superstar challengers!

The Hounds of Justice do it again. Can anyone beat this outstanding Tag Team?

Roman Reigns celebrates his Tag Team's victory!

The Shield really have shown the WWE Universe what it means to dish out true justice. Victory once more for The Shield! What a match!

JOHN CENA®

John Cena came to WrestleMania XXX in order to prove to the WWE Universe that Bray Wyatt could not bring out the beast in him... and, of course, he also came to win! Bray's mind games played havoc with Cena's game plan from the very start of this epic battle, and the interference of both Harper and Rowan hindered Cena greatly in his mission to finish Wyatt quickly. Despite this, Cena battled the demons that Bray attempted to invoke inside him and eventually summoned the honour and strength within him to become victorious over his strange and macabre opponent.

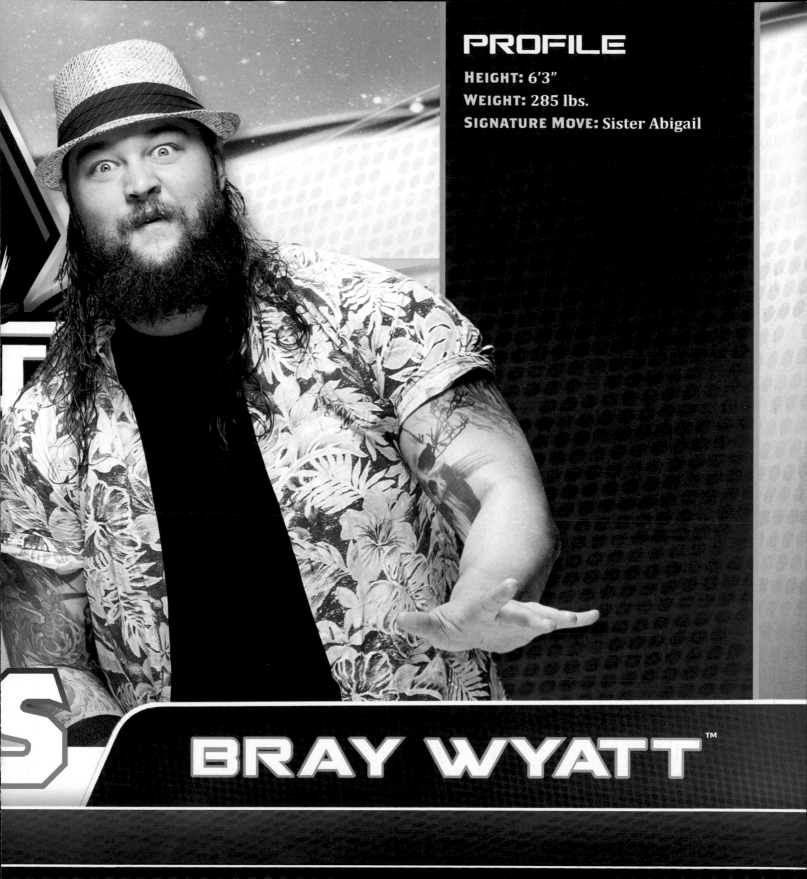

PROFILE

HEIGHT: 6'3"
WEIGHT: 285 lbs.
SIGNATURE MOVE: Sister Abigail

BRAY WYATT ™

Bray Wyatt was determined to expose Cena for what he thought he really was from the moment he stepped into the WWE arena! His every look; his every movement; his every sound was chosen deliberately in order to shake the inner darkness out of his opponent, eventually weakening him enough for Bray's brutally bizarre, yet devastating, moves to do the rest! Unfortunately for Bray however, Cena's will was far stronger than he had expected, and in the end he fell to the superior skills of his foe!

As a spooky looking masked band plays, Bray, holding a lantern to light his way, takes the long walk down the ramp.

Accompanied by Erick Rowan and Luke Harper, Bray kneels on the canvas and, with a crazed look in his eye, laps up the energy of the WWE arena.

Despite Bray's earlier confidence, it's clear from his face that Cena's presence has already unsettled him!

Then comes John Cena, with a look of pure concentration and determination etched on his face!

Cena, on the other hand, doesn't look phased at all!

As the bell sounds, Wyatt kneels and screams 'Finish me'! Cena responds by immediately taking him down and immobilizing with a side headlock!

Despite this, Wyatt comes back... beating and stomping on Cena!

Once on his feet, Wyatt shows no mercy to Cena, putting him right back down with a vicious clothesline.

Once up, as Wyatt winds up to finish Cena, Cena smashes him with a massive clothesline, reaffirming his and the crowds belief in his ability to win!

Grabbing Cena by his head, Wyatt screams 'This is the one you call hero?'

For a few moments Cena stands by the ropes to catch his breath... but then he turns and the Bray-beating begins!

Wyatt tries to laugh off the attack, but the beatings continue...

... the intensity of Cena's strikes making the referee pull him back!

Cena pulls Wyatt up and hits him with a huge elbow, sending him down once more.

Wyatt, despite this turn of events, is still smiling!

Cena then sends a monstrous kick to the face of The Wyatt family's front man!

Wyatt gets back to his feet and retaliates, slamming Cena and screaming 'I know you John!' as he begins to pummel the Superstar.

Wyatt drags Cena to his feet, harshly, by his ears...

After escaping a chokehold, Cena hits Wyatt with a devastating shoulder tackle...

... then picks him up...

... and slams him onto the canvas like Wyatt were a rag doll!

With Wyatt down, Cena smells blood... and with it... victory!

As Cena goes to finish his challenger, Wyatt stuns him with some seriously weird Wyatt moves...

allowing Wyatt to grab Cena and slam him to the canvas!

... but Wyatt has other plans!

Wyatt unsuccessfully goes for the pin...

... but once outside the ropes he executes a vicious face-first DDT on the Cenation leader.

Cena recovers and to the surprise of everyone, not least Wyatt, leaps from the top ropes onto Rowan and Harper, smashing them to the ground!

Wyatt retaliates, throwing Cena into the metal steps and picking them up with destruction on his mind!

But Cena summons his reserves and pounds Wyatt before being hit by the steps.

Once back in the ring, Wyatt hits Cena with a big shoulder and goes for another pin... but fails.

Wyatt then throws Cena through the ropes, but Cena fires back by smashing Harper through the barricade and into the timekeeper's area!

Cena and Wyatt battle on, Wyatt becoming more and more outraged at Cena's refusal to let the monster out...

...but Cena refuses, instead opting to use the last of his strength to lift Wyatt and execute a huge AA, finishing the Wyatt family front man with a pin.

Visibly emotional by the win, Cena takes in the adoring cheers from the WWE crowd...

... then leaves the ring with his head held high...

... and wastes no time in showing his fans just how grateful he is for their support!

Cena leaves the arena, secure in the knowledge that he defeated the influence of Wyatt... with honour!

PROFILE

HEIGHT: 6'3"
WEIGHT: 286 lbs.
FROM: Minneapolis, Minn.
SIGNATURE MOVE: F-5; Kimura Lock
CAREER HIGHLIGHTS: WWE Champion; 2002 King of the Ring; 2003 Royal Rumble Match winner; Ending Undertaker's WrestleMania Streak

BROCK LESNAR

Brock Lesnar came to *WrestleMania XXX* for one reason, – to break the undefeated *WrestleMania* streak of the immortal, the legendary, Undertaker! Not only did The Beast Incarnate complete this almost unthinkable mission, but he did it within a match that will surely go down in WWE history as one of the greatest matches ever to be fought within **WWE**. With massively powerful, bone-crunching moves executed by both gigantic Superstars, it will be a long time before anyone is able to top this spectacular battle! Despite a valiant effort by the great Undertaker, Brock actually did 'Eat, sleep, conquer the streak'!

PROFILE

HEIGHT: 6'10"

WEIGHT: 299 lbs.

FROM: Death Valley

SIGNATURE MOVE: Chokeslam; Tombstone; Last Ride

CAREER HIGHLIGHTS:
WWE Champion; World Heavyweight Champion; World Tag Team Champion; WCW Tag Team Champion; Hardcore Champion

UNDERTAKER®

With a *WrestleMania* record of 21:0, Undertaker came to New Orleans with no plans of losing his winning streak to his archrival, The Beast Incarnate. However, victory for The Deadman was not to be, and in a battle that shook the WWE Universe, despite using every skill at his disposal to eliminate this brute of an adversary, in the end the youth and sheer strength of Brock Lesnar was too much even for this legend of WWE!

The Beast Incarnate, Brock Lesnar, stands ready, his massive frame dwarfing that of his manager...

... and as he makes his way down the ramp, he definitely DOES NOT look like a man who came here to lose!

Now it's the turn of 'The Phenom', the Undertaker. His sheer presence bringing an eerie quiet over the entire WWE arena!

Brock, however, does not look intimidated!

As they meet face to face, the two giants stare coldly into each other's eyes...

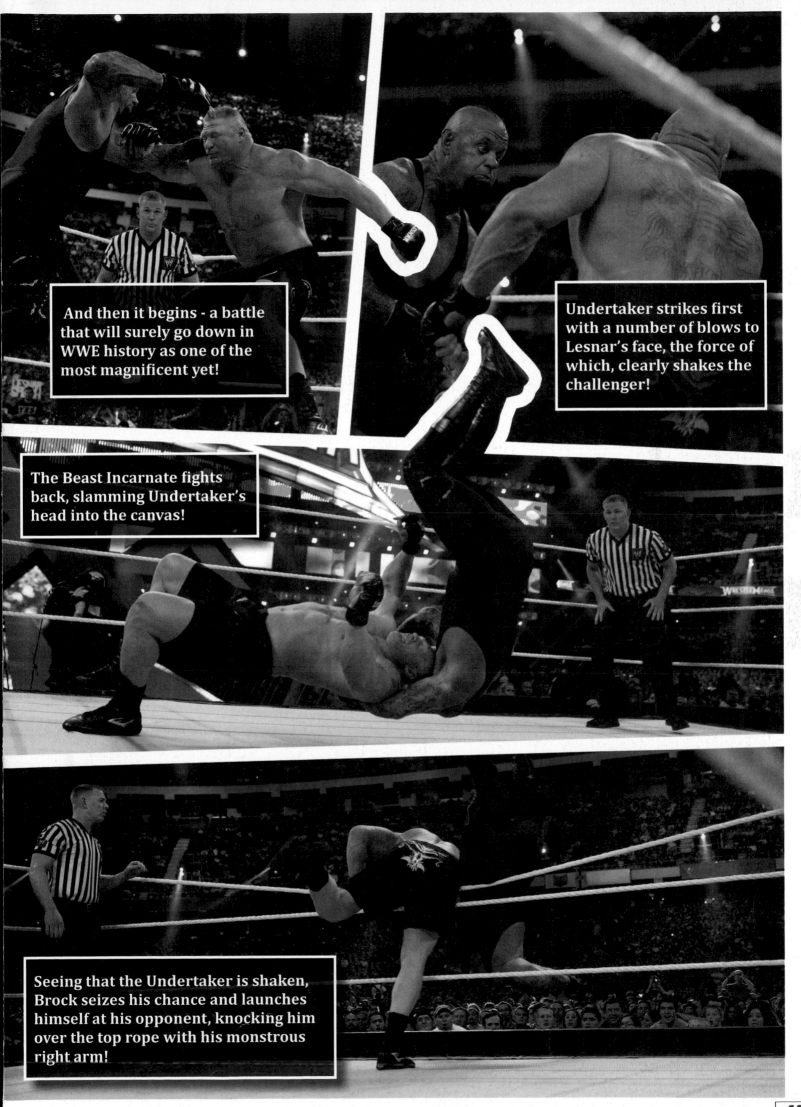

And then it begins - a battle that will surely go down in WWE history as one of the most magnificent yet!

Undertaker strikes first with a number of blows to Lesnar's face, the force of which, clearly shakes the challenger!

The Beast Incarnate fights back, slamming Undertaker's head into the canvas!

Seeing that the Undertaker is shaken, Brock seizes his chance and launches himself at his opponent, knocking him over the top rope with his monstrous right arm!

Undertaker, still on his feet, stares back at Lesnar, with sheer hatred in his eyes!

Undertaker hits back with some solid strikes to Lesnar's face.

Once back in the ring, Undertaker once again begins to batter Lesnar into the corner post.

Then follows Brock out as he tries to escape and slams his head into the corner post...

...rocking the Beast Incarnate!

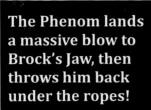

The Phenom lands a massive blow to Brock's Jaw, then throws him back under the ropes!

Undertaker takes control of the match with blistering, merciless moves...

... winding up...

...and unleashing a brutal chokeslam on The Beast!

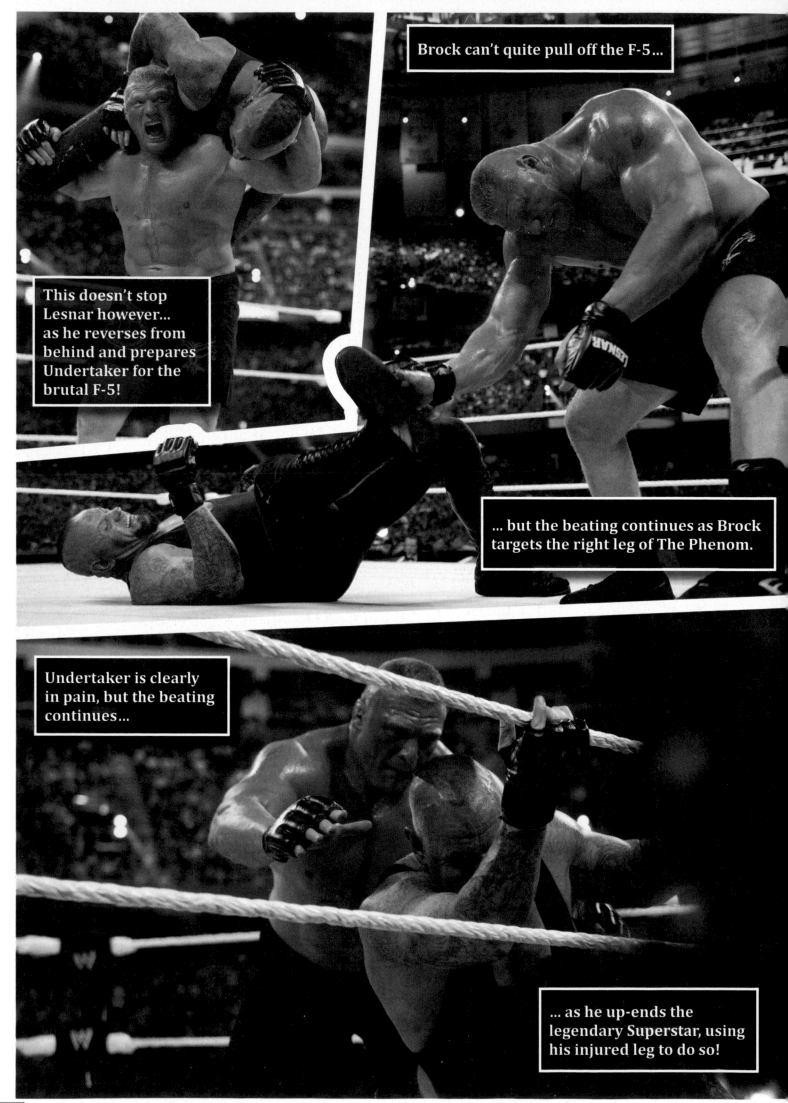

Brock can't quite pull off the F-5...

This doesn't stop Lesnar however... as he reverses from behind and prepares Undertaker for the brutal F-5!

... but the beating continues as Brock targets the right leg of The Phenom.

Undertaker is clearly in pain, but the beating continues...

... as he up-ends the legendary Superstar, using his injured leg to do so!

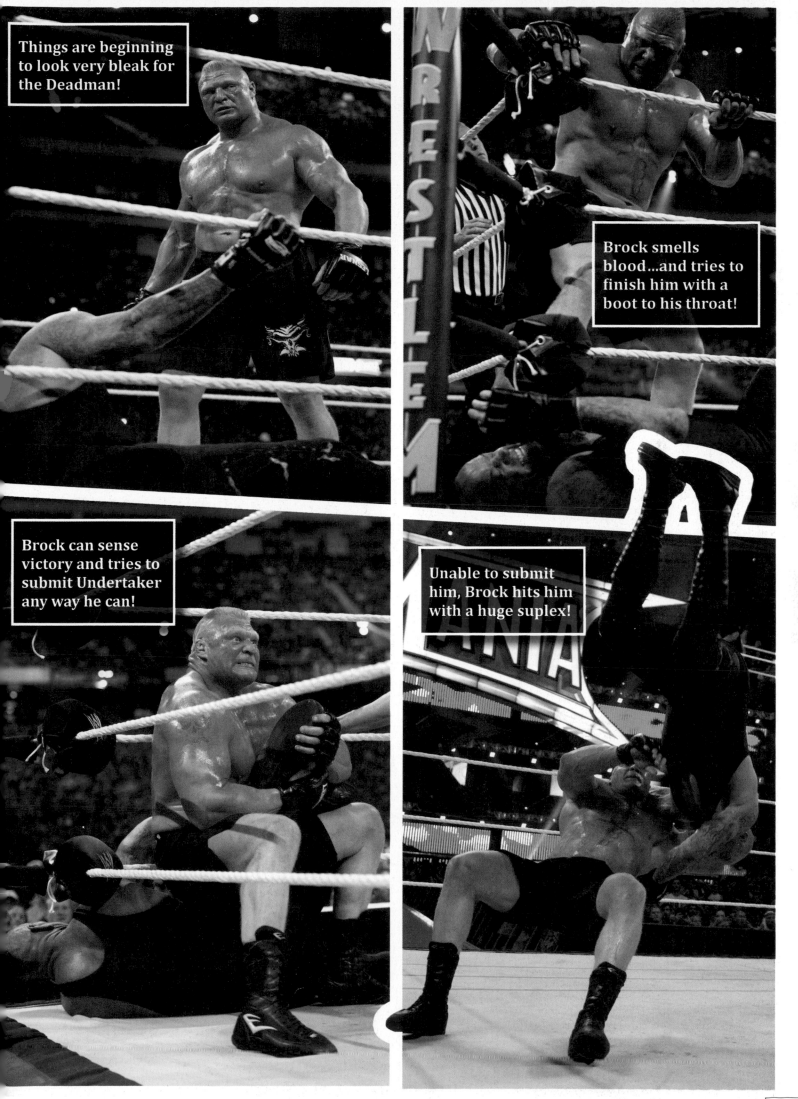

Things are beginning to look very bleak for the Deadman!

Brock smells blood...and tries to finish him with a boot to his throat!

Brock can sense victory and tries to submit Undertaker any way he can!

Unable to submit him, Brock hits him with a huge suplex!

Lesnar unleashes his fury onto the battered body of Undertaker...

... but Undertaker counters with a perfect DDT, buying himself critical time to recover!

Undertaker then executes a snake-eyes, and hits Lesnar hard with a high boot!

Smashing Brock with a leg drop, Undertaker goes for the pin... but Brock kicks out!

Undeterred, The Phenom grabs Lesnar and performs a spectacular chokeslam on The Beast...!

Undertaker tries to pin Lesnar again but again the challenger kicks out!

As though summoning power from the Gods,...Lesnar comes back and slams Undertaker with a monstrous F-5...

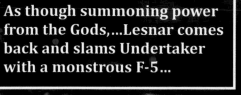

Just as all hope seems lost for Undertaker, he grabs Lesnar... and goes for a Hell's Gate, in an attempt to force the tap!

The two men battle ferociously despite being exhausted, neither man willing to give up!

Brock has other ideas however, lifting Undertaker... and slamming him onto his back! Could this really be the end of 'The Streak'?

Once back on their feet, Undertaker lifts Brock and slams him onto his back...

Undertaker looks for the pin, but is denied by Brock!

... before picking him up again and drilling him into the canvas with a tombstone piledriver!

Getting to his feet, The Deadman signals the end for Lesnar...

... but Lesnar counters with his hardest F-5 yet, incapacitating The Phenom, winning the match...

... and breaking the Streak that most had come to believe was unbreakable!

In a battle to match any battle ever fought in WWE, Brock Lesnar has shocked the WWE Universe, and emerged victorious!

BATISTA

HEIGHT: 6'6"
WEIGHT: 278 lbs.
FROM: Washington, D.C.
SIGNATURE MOVE: Batista Bomb
NICKNAME: The Animal

RANDY ORTON

HEIGHT: 6'5"
WEIGHT: 245 lbs.
FROM: St. Louis, Mo.
SIGNATURE MOVE: RKO
NICKNAME: The Viper

TRIPLE THREAT MATCH

FOR

Batista came to *WrestleMania XXX* to win, not to make friends, yet despite putting on a great show for the crowd, The Animal simply could not break down the courage and resolve of Daniel Bryan, this failure eventually making the massive Superstar leave the stadium having done neither!

Randy Orton was the WWE World Heavyweight Champion when he arrived at *WrestleMania XXX*, but Daniel Bryan soon showed him he is not the only one who knows what it takes

THE WORLD HEAVYWEIGHT CHAMPIONSHIP

to be a true Champion! Despite numerous RKO attempts, and a number of underhanded tactics, the Viper was taught a lesson by Bryan, which he isn't likely to forget for many years to come!

Daniel Bryan came to *WrestleMania XXX* with an injured shoulder, which makes his defeats over Triple H, Batista, and Randy Orton even more spectacular! If this stunningly talented Superstar can take on the best and win, when handicapped by injury, just imagine what he will achieve in the rest of his career at WWE! Daniel Bryan is most definitely a legend in the making!

Next to make his entrance is The Animal, Batista...

The Viper arrives at the ring, pumped and ready for action... as the crowd goes crazy for their WWE World Heavyweight Champion, Randy Orton!

...and he's looking as big, and as bad as ever!

Last but not least, with a clearly injured left shoulder, Daniel Bryan enters the arena... his 'Yes' Movement cheering their challenger and giving him all the support they can, in order to help him battle on through his pain.

52

As the bell rings, Daniel Bryan takes no time in attacking the current champ...

Batista takes advantage of Bryan's distraction and grabs him...but Bryan is able to counter and, to The Animal's amazement, throws him through the ropes!

... launching himself at The Viper with a massive flying kick!

... and executes a devastating backbreaker on his adversary!

Back in the ring, Batista quickly wipes the smile from Orton's face... but within seconds the Champion turns the tables on The Beast...

The Beast gets up quickly however, slamming The Viper out of the ring and pounding him into the edge of the mat!

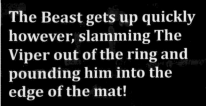

Batista prepares to deliver a Batista Bomb on his stunned opponent, but Orton counters, slamming The Animal's back into the steal steps...

Batista then smashes Orton into the announcer's table, leaving the Champ dazed on the floor!

... the pain clear to see on Superstar's face!

With Batista down, Orton sets his sights on the injured Daniel Bryan...

... and slams him into the barricade, once again taking the 'Yes!' Movement man out of the equation!

Orton drags Batista back into the ring, but just as he thinks he's winning the match...

... Daniel Bryan, as if from nowhere, launches himself from the top rope...

... flooring both Superstars with a massive double missile drop kick! Despite injuring his shoulder further with the fall...

... Daniel Bryan, with a chant of 'Yes!' from the arena, sets about landing kick after kick on the bewildered Superstars kneeling before him!

Just as Bryan senses victory however, Orton summons the strength to pick him up...

... and slams him, hard, onto his injured shoulder!

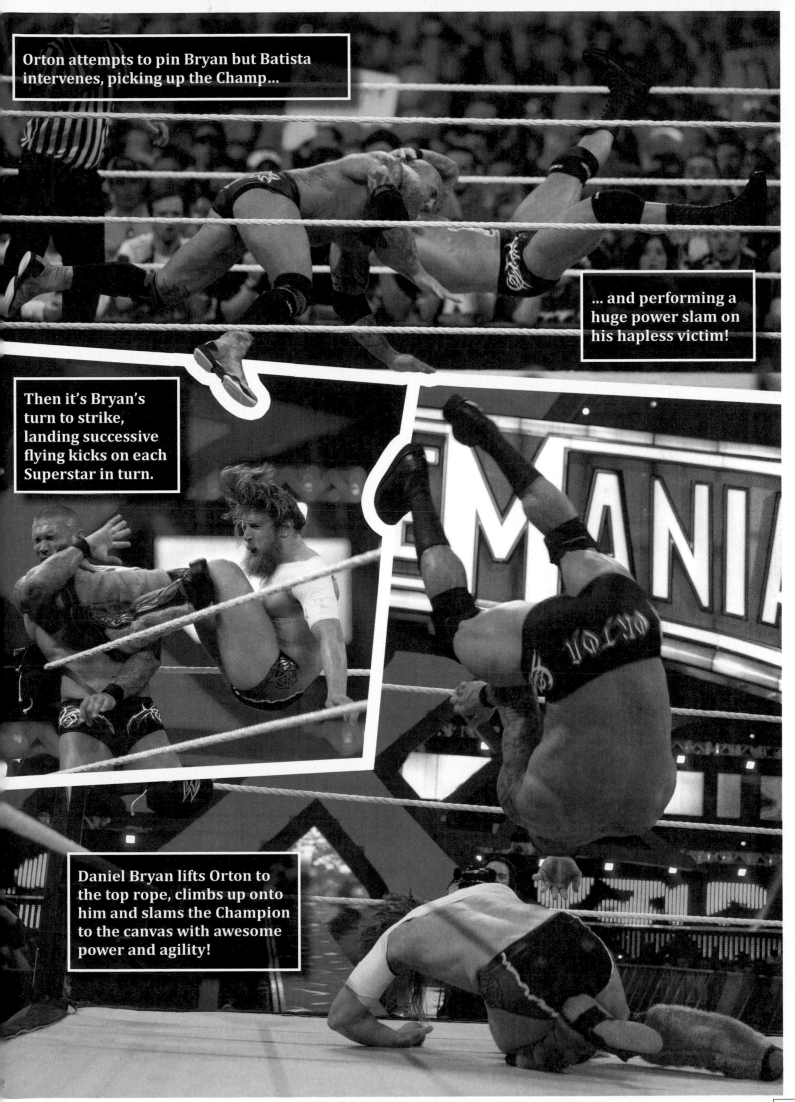

Orton attempts to pin Bryan but Batista intervenes, picking up the Champ...

... and performing a huge power slam on his hapless victim!

Then it's Bryan's turn to strike, landing successive flying kicks on each Superstar in turn.

Daniel Bryan lifts Orton to the top rope, climbs up onto him and slams the Champion to the canvas with awesome power and agility!

... but Orton sees the danger. Then, with a roar of appreciation from the crowd, Randy Orton executes a dazzling Superplex on the challenger, stunning both Superstars as they hit the canvas!

After throwing an exhausted Bryan to the outside, Batista mounts the turnbuckle and prepares to leap on Orton...

Once again, as if from nowhere, Daniel Bryan comes flying through the air towards the downed giants... and lands heavily on the Champion!
Bryan then goes for the pin, but due to the underhanded antics of Triple H (who dragged the ref out of the ring) the count cannot be completed.

... just as Stephanie makes an unexpected appearance herself!

Batista makes the most of this distraction and executes a devastating Spinebuster on Daniel Bryan...

Batista focuses once more on Daniel Bryan, whilst Triple H sends a corrupt referee, by the name of Scott Armstrong, into the ring, in place of the one he has just injured.

Batista continues his onslaught on the "Yes!" Movement' front man, with a devastating Batista Bomb... clearly hurting the exhausted and injured Superstar!

Despite his injury, Bryan manages to kick out of the pin attempt... denying Triple H's effort to fix the match! Bryan leaps through the ropes, taking out 'The Authority', before getting back on the canvas and taking on The Animal and The Viper once more.

As Bryan is immobilized by a Batista Bomb (into an RKO), leaving him in a neck brace, The Animal and The Viper battle it out alone!

But wait... Bryan refuses medical attention and is back in the match, dodging another RKO and narrowly missing a win via a 'Yes! Lock' on the Champion.

Batista tries desperately to make Orton tap, as Bryan recovers at the corner...

... but the tables quickly turn as Orton narrowly misses a tap from Batista, after a brutal RKO.

Batista retaliates on Orton with a Batista Bomb but for the third time in this epic battle Daniel Brian comes from nowhere with a massive knee... flooring Batista and enabling Bryan to trap him in his signature 'Yes! Lock' submission move!

Within mere moments Batista taps out and Daniel Bryan achieves his ultimate goal – becoming the WWE World Heavyweight Champion!

ROUND UP AND ALL RESULTS FROM ALL MATCHES

Winner of Brock Lesnar Vs Undertaker: *Brock Lesnar*

Winner of John Cena Vs Bray Wyatt: *John Cena*

Winner of Daniel Bryan Vs Triple H: *Daniel Bryan*

Winner of the 'Andre the Giant Memorial Battle Royal': *Cesaro!*

**Winner of the Six-Man Tag Team match, between
The Shield & The New Age Outlaws (*plus Kane*):** *The Shield*

**Winners of the Pre-Show Fatal 4-Way Match -
The Usos vs Los Matadores (*Diego and Fernando*)
vs The Real Americans (*Cesaro and Jack Swagger*)
vs RybAxel (*Ryback and Curtis Axel*):
WWE Tag Team Champions:** *The Usos*

**Winner of the Vickie Guerrero
Divas Championship Invitational, 14-Diva,
single-fall match for the
WWE Divas Championship:** *AJ Lee*